Marigold
the
Goldfish

The Animal Friends Books

Marigold the Goldfish

by
Margaret Sanford Pursell

CAROLRHODA BOOKS
MINNEAPOLIS, MINNESOTA U.S.A.

Revised English text by Margaret Sanford Pursell. Original French text by Anne-Marie Pajot. Translation by Dyan Hammarberg. Photographs by Pierre Michel Rapho. Drawings by L'Enc Matte.

LIBRARY OF CONGRESS CATALOGING IN PUBLICATION DATA

Pursell, Margaret Sanford.
  Marigold the goldfish.

  (The Animal Friends Books)
  Original ed. published under title: Glob, le poisson rouge.
  SUMMARY: A young boy learns about the care of aquarium fish when he buys some goldfish and an aquarium.

  1. Goldfish—Juvenile literature. [1. Goldfish. 2. Aquariums] I. Pajot, Anne Marie. Glob, le poisson rouge. II. Rapho, Pierre Michel. III. Matte, L'Enc. IV. Title.

  SF458.G6P87 1976   639'.34   76-1213
  ISBN 0-87614-065-7

First published in the United States of America 1976 by Carolrhoda Books, Inc. All English language rights reserved.

Original edition published by Librairie A. Hatier, Paris, France, under the title GLOB LE POISSON ROUGE. English text and drawings © 1976 Carolrhoda Books, Inc. Photographs © 1974 Librairie A. Hatier.

Manufactured in the United States of America. Published simultaneously in Canada by J. M. Dent & Sons (Canada) Ltd., Don Mills, Ontario.

International Standard Book Number: 0-87614-065-7
Library of Congress Catalog Card Number: 76-1213

Whenever he gets the chance, Chris hurries down the street to Boisey's Pet Store to look at the wonderful animals. He loves to spend hours at a time watching the animals and imagining what it would be like to have a pet of his own. He sees puppies, kittens, hamsters, parakeets, and brilliantly colored tropical fish. There are also talking parrots, monkeys, and lizards that change color. But of all the animals in the store, Chris is most fascinated by the fish. They are so graceful and pretty as they swim in and out among the water plants. One day, Chris comes into Boisey's not just to pass the time, but to buy something for himself—some fish and an aquarium.

Chris walks past the rows of tanks trying to decide what kind of fish to get. He looks at guppies, mollies, swordtails, and zebrafish. And there are catfish, angelfish, neon tetras, and goldfish. With so many different kinds to choose from, it will be hard for him to decide. Mr. Boisey comes over to help.

"Goldfish are always nice to start out with," he says. "They're pretty fish, and they're also easy to take care of."

After thinking it over for a while, Chris decides to take Mr. Boisey's advice. They scoop a few goldfish out of the tank with a net and put them in plastic bags filled with water. Then Mr. Boisey helps Chris pick out an aquarium and some equipment.

Net

Thermometer

Water Heater

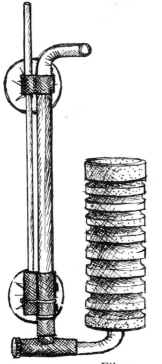

Filter

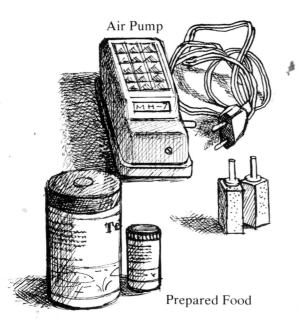

Air Pump

Prepared Food

To give the goldfish lots of room to swim in and plenty of oxygen to breathe, they choose a large rectangular tank. Chris is surprised at how much other equipment he will need in order to set up his aquarium. First, he will need a water heater. Because most tropical fish are used to living in warm water, the water in the tank must be kept at 72 degrees. A thermostat and thermometer are also needed to help Chris keep the temperature of the water just right.

Then, to make sure that the fish get enough oxygen, Chris will need an air pump. This small machine pumps bubbles of air into the water, making it easier for the fish to breathe. Attached to the air pump is a filter that helps to keep the water clean.

As soon as Chris gets home, he starts to prepare the aquarium. First, he takes the tank into the garden and scoops some soil into it. Mr. Boisey says that a thin layer of dirt on the bottom of the tank will help the plants to grow. Then Chris washes the gravel that Mr. Boisey has given him and spreads it over the soil.

Now Chris is ready to add water to the tank, but he must wait to add the plants and fish. Mr. Boisey tells him that tap water must *age*, or stand in the tank for a while, before it will be safe to use.

"There are chemicals in tap water that are harmful to tropical fish," says Mr. Boisey. "But if you let the water stand for a few days, most of the chemicals will disappear."

For the next few days, Chris keeps the goldfish in a large, clear bowl. The fish are very frisky after being cooped up in a plastic bag for so long, and they swim back and forth briskly. One fish presses its mouth against the glass and seems to look at Chris. This fish is a deeper gold than the rest—it is almost orange, like the color of marigolds in summer. Chris decides to name his brightly colored fish Marigold, after the flower.

Marigold and the other goldfish glide easily through the water with their smooth, streamlined bodies. By waving their tails from side to side, they move around each other in graceful swirls. All the while, their fins are helping them to balance, to turn, or to just stay still.

Chris is amazed to see the fish continually gulping water. Their mouths open and close as though they are eating bits of things in the water. But what the goldfish are actually doing is breathing. By taking water into their mouths, the fish are also moving water over their *gills*. Gills are special organs that take oxygen from the water. They are located underneath the rounded slits on either side of a fish's head.

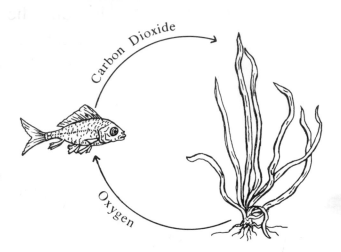

When the water has finished aging, Chris can finally put his fish in the aquarium. But first, he must add the plants. Plants will play a very important part in the underwater world that Chris is making. In addition to being beautiful, plants will provide shade and shelter for the fish. They will also help to provide enough oxygen for the fish to breathe.

Chris wants many different kinds of plants in his aquarium to make it look like a beautiful underwater garden. The plants at Boisey's have long scientific names that are hard to pronounce, but Chris knows which ones he wants. He gets some that are wispy, some that are thick and bushy, and some that are like tall grass. In all, he gets six different kinds. Being careful not to churn up the water, he plants them in the gravel, using a long stick. Then he places a few smooth rocks on the bottom of the aquarium for decoration. The tank is very beautiful now, even without the fish. And it should provide everything the goldfish will need—heat, oxygen, light, and shelter.

Before Chris adds the fish to the tank, he checks to make sure that the temperature of the water is exactly 72 degrees. Then he puts the fish in a jar, seals it, and floats it in the aquarium. This will give the fish a chance to adjust themselves to the temperature of the water in the tank. Unlike people, fish are *cold-blooded* creatures—their body temperature adjusts itself to the temperature of their surroundings. But fish can only adjust to a gradual change in temperature. If the temperature of the water around them changes suddenly, the fish may get sick and die.

Elodea   Cabomba   Ludwigia   Myriophyllum   Aponogeton   Sagittaria

After about an hour, Chris takes the fish out of the jar and lets them swim freely in the tank. At last Marigold and the other goldfish are in their new home.

Chris takes good care of his fish and aquarium. Three times a day, he feeds the goldfish a pinch of prepared food. And once in a while, he gives them a bit of frozen shrimp or crab. Then Marigold and the other goldfish streak to the top of the tank to devour the juicy tidbits. But Chris is careful not to give the fish too much to eat. Mr. Boisey says that uneaten food will decay in the water and make it dirty.

When the sides of the tank get mossy-looking, Chris scrapes them off with a special scraping tool. And every now and then he cleans the bottom of the tank with a *dip tube* that sucks up particles of dirt.

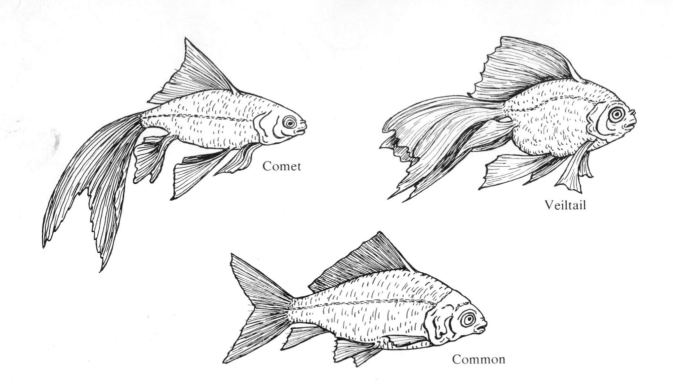

Comet

Veiltail

Common

    Except for slight differences in color, Marigold and the other goldfish in Chris' tank are all alike. They are called common goldfish. But there are many other varieties of goldfish that Chris will want to have in his tank someday. Some goldfish, like the veiltail or the comet, have long, trailing tails and fins. Others, like the shubunkin, are not a gold color at all. The shubunkin is actually a shimmering blue, with spots of red and yellow. Chris will have a hard time convincing his friends that a blue fish is a *goldfish*! Other kinds of goldfish are too large to keep in a tank at home. These are kept in large pools outside, like the one at the park. There, the goldfish will have plenty of room to swim and play. Some of them will grow to be as large as 12 inches long.

Having an aquarium is a new and exciting experience for Chris. But the idea of aquariums is actually very old—people have been keeping fish in pools or tanks for hundreds of years. Long ago, Romans kept fish in shallow pools, much like miniature ponds, right in their homes. And the Chinese have been raising goldfish for nearly a thousand years.

Today, having an aquarium can be more exciting than ever before. Tanks are better equipped to provide everything a fish will need—heat, oxygen, and light. And modern airplanes and ships can bring brilliantly colored tropical fish from all over the world to be sold at pet stores like Boisey's. Even fish from the ocean—like the one in this picture—can be kept in special saltwater tanks. It's very difficult to keep a saltwater aquarium, but maybe someday Chris will want to give it a try. He has had such good luck with Marigold and the other goldfish that he bought at Boisey's Pet Store.

DO YOU KNOW . . .

- the name for fish that are newly born or hatched?

- how fish are able to swim in the dark?

- why goldfish do not survive long in natural surroundings?

TO FIND THE ANSWERS TO THESE QUESTIONS,
TURN THE PAGE 👉

FACTS ABOUT GOLDFISH

Goldfish are one of 21,000 different kinds of fish. Like all other fish, they have backbones, they breathe with gills, and they are *cold-blooded*. Cold-blooded animals have body temperatures that adjust to the temperature of their surroundings.

Goldfish belong to a family of fish known as carp. Nearly a thousand years ago, the Chinese bred—or mated—ordinary carp that lived in the lakes and streams. These early experiments with breeding led to the creation of a new, brightly colored variety of carp—goldfish.

Fish have two different methods of reproduction. Some fish bear their young fully formed, or alive. Other fish, including goldfish, lay eggs. Fish that are newly born or hatched are called *fries.* These baby fish are so tiny that adult fish sometimes try to eat them.

goldfish fry
(enlarged to show detail)

All types of fish have a dark stripe that runs down either side of their bodies. This stripe, called the *lateral line,* is made up of special nerve endings that enable fish to "feel" the slightest movement in the water around them. The lateral line helps fish to swim in the dark without bumping into things and to know when larger fish are approaching.

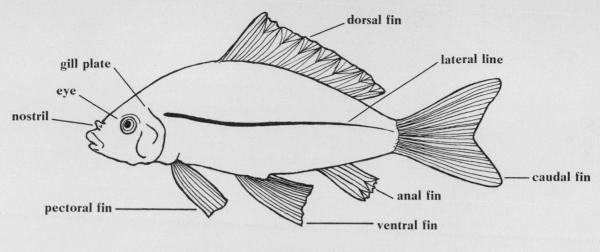

DIAGRAM OF A GOLDFISH

Because goldfish have eyes on either side of their heads, they are able to see in two directions at the same time. Goldfish are also able to hear, smell, and feel many different things.

Goldfish eat both plants and animals—they are *omnivorous* (om-NIV-ur-us). In addition to nibbling on the plants in an aquarium, goldfish will also eat prepared foods, bits of meat, and fish.

Goldfish that are kept in aquariums usually grow to be one or two inches long, not including their tails. But goldfish that are kept in very large tanks or in ponds outside will grow to be much larger. Despite their increased size, goldfish that live outside do not have a very good chance of surviving. Their brilliant colors and unusual fins attract *predators*—animals that will try to eat them.

The Animal Friends Books

Clover the CALF

Jessie the CHICKEN

Ali the DESERT FOX

Splash the DOLPHIN

Dolly the DONKEY

Downy the DUCKLING

ELEPHANTS around the World

Tippy the FOX TERRIER

Marigold the GOLDFISH

Polly the GUINEA PIG

Winslow the HAMSTER

Figaro the HORSE

Rusty the IRISH SETTER

Boots the KITTEN

Penny and Pete the LAMBS

The LIONS of Africa

Mandy the MONKEY

Lorito the PARROT

Curly the PIGLET

Whiskers the RABBIT

Shelley the SEA GULL

Penelope the TORTOISE

Sprig the TREE FROG

Tanya the TURTLE DOVE

CAROLRHODA BOOKS

241 FIRST AVENUE NORTH — MINNEAPOLIS, MINNESOTA 55401

Published in memory of Carolrhoda Locketz Rozell,
Who loved to bring children and books together

Please write for a complete catalogue